Making Memories

Janette Oke

ILLUSTRATED BY Cheri Bladholm

BETHANY
BACKYARD®
MINNEAPOLIS, MN 55438

Making Memories

Text copyright © 1999 by Janette Oke.
Illustrations copyright © 1999 by Cheri Bladholm.

Design and production by Lookout Design Group, Inc. (www.lookoutdesign.com)
Printed in Italy.

Library of Congress Cataloging-in-Publication Data
CIP applied for

I will praise thee; for I am fearfully and
wonderfully made: marvelous are thy works....

—PSALM 139:14a KJV

To Conner Edward Oke,
with love from Grandma

—JANETTE OKE

My warmest thanks to Simon Roehrich and his
grandfather Michel Settia of Valence, France,
who modeled for the characters in this story.
And thanks also to Greg Tharp, the photographer
who captured their mutual affection—exactly
the inspiration I needed to paint.

—CHERI BLADHOLM

"Grandpa...how do you make memories?"

"Well, now..." said Grandpa, stroking his chin. "Just what do you have in mind, Joel?"

"I'm not sure. Grandma said, 'Thank God for His gift of memories. The things we enjoy, we can relive again and again.'"

"Oh, I see." Grandpa nodded and reached out a hand to me. "Come here," he said, "and I'll tell you the secret."

4

I leaned against Grandpa's knee. His arm slipped around my shoulder and pulled me close. I felt like the baby chicks when they peek out from under their mother's wing.

"What you've got to do," said Grandpa, "is pay particular attention to everything that goes on around you." Grandpa lifted a hand and pointed a finger at his eyes. "Gotta use these," he said.

I let my eyes slide out over the porch— all the way across the yard, past the red barn with the tall rooster weather vane, on over the fields, the trees, the creek, and the distant hills. But Grandpa brought my far-off attention quickly back.

"See that itty bitty frog?"

I looked where Grandpa's big, work-roughened hand was pointing. A little green frog with funny spots on his back was hopping toward the garden.

"And look up there. Way up. See that bird so high up in the clouds that he looks like a speck against the sky? That's a hawk. Out to see what's going on in God's big world."

I had to squint my eyes almost shut to see the hawk against the white fluffiness of the clouds.

I looked back at Grandpa. I thought I understood.

"So...making memories is...seeing things?"

Grandpa nodded, his favorite cap bobbing up and down on his gray hair. "That's the first part."

I leaned a little closer against his knee.

"You have to see—and all the other things," went on Grandpa.

"What other things?"

He pointed at his nose, then took a noisy sniff. "I can tell Grandma is getting our dinner ready. Smells to me like spicy apple pie for dessert."

At first I could smell nothing. Nothing but the rich, deep, woodsy smell of Grandpa's jacket.

Then I stepped back and sniffed. Now I could smell apple pie, too. Tangy. Sweet. I could hardly wait for dinner.

Grandpa turned the other way and breathed in again. "Smell the hay," he told me. "Your dad is cutting the west field. Clover. Love the smell of newly cut clover."

I took a deep breath. Fresh clover. It made me think of lambs playing in the fields, butting heads in pretend battles.

Grandpa turned his head slightly and tapped at an ear. "Gotta use these, too."

I reached up and felt my ear. Mama always said that I had my daddy's ears.

"Listen," said Grandpa. "What do you hear?"

At first I couldn't hear anything special because of the noises. The old porch chair creaked when Grandpa shifted his weight. One of his work shoes scraped across the wooden porch boards, making a scuffling sound. Sparky, my dog, barked at a squirrel. All the nearby noises made it hard to listen.

In the branches, there was the whisper of a buzzing sound from a bumblebee hunting for pollen. From the far-off pasture came soft mooing as a cow called to her calf. The hum of the distant tractor told me where my dad was working.

"There's more to the secret, Joel," Grandpa continued. "You've gotta use these, too," he said, holding up one of his hands.

Grandpa rubbed the big, gentle hand over my head. "I think I'd know it was you—even in the dark," he said. "Just by the way your hair feels."

I reached up and rubbed my hair. It sort of stuck out funny, even though Mama made me comb it. I smacked it down with the palm of my hand. It bounced right up again.

"We can read things through our fingers," Grandpa explained.

I squinted up at Grandpa, then looked down at my hands. How could I read with my fingers?

"Shut your eyes," said Grandpa.

I shut them. The whole world was gone in a blink.

"Now reach out a hand."

I held out my hand—but it was a little scary.

Something touched the palm of my hand. I jumped and tried to pull my hand back, but Grandpa held my hand in his.

"What is it?" I whispered.

I waited—then let my fingers curl
over the item in my hand.

I could tell it was the jackknife that he used to
cut willow branches to make whistles, or to slice
twine to tie up something. One of the blades he
used only for peeling an apple out of the buckets
he filled when he was working in the garden.

"Your jackknife." I laughed and opened my eyes.
"That's easy."

"You saw with your fingers, Joel," Grandpa told me,
a smile in his voice. "Close your eyes again."

He placed another something in my hand. It was
small and round and hard. I could feel faint markings—
and warmth. Warmth from being deep in Grandpa's
pants' pocket.

"A coin. A dime maybe."

"Good," said Grandpa. "But your hands don't just
tell you things when you have your eyes closed. They
tell you things all day long."

I leaned against the smooth hardness of the chair arm.

"Have you ever been shopping with your grandma?"

I nodded. Many times.

"Have you seen her use her hands?"

I thought real hard. In my mind I could see Grandma picking up soft fabric, running it through her fingers.

I nodded to Grandpa.

"Your fingers tell you things, too. Like when a fish is on the line."

I could almost feel the sensation of the pole pulling against the tightness of my hand.

"Or which tomato to bring in off the vine when Grandma sends you for one."

The ready tomatoes were soft to the touch, leaving little dents when I pressed my thumb against their redness.

"Thanks, Grandpa," I said, eager to be off to work on some memories of my own.

"Not so fast," said Grandpa with a chuckle. "We still haven't talked about the second part of the secret."

"Second part?"

"It's very important," said Grandpa, and he tapped a finger against his forehead. "The first part is to pay close attention. Really notice God's world around you using eyes, nose, ears, hands. The second part is to store all of that—up here."

I squinted up at him again. How would I store it all?

"It's not so hard," went on Grandpa. "In fact, God made our brain so it kind of does the work on its own."

I still didn't know what he meant.

"What was the most exciting thing that happened to you this last year?"

I scratched my head. Christmas was exciting. Celebrating the birth of Baby Jesus at Aunt Mary and Uncle John's.

But my birthday was good, too. I got my very first bike. It was shiny blue, with wide tires and streamers that waved out from the handlebars when I went fast down the lane.

"It's hard to decide, isn't it?" said Grandpa as he waited for my answer.

I nodded.

"What about the last time we went fishing?"

Oh—I remembered that   day!   The sky was so blue. I wished I could fly up into its blueness. And the sun was so warm on my back it felt like Mama's hand. But the creek was cool. We let our feet dip into the wetness, wriggling our toes to watch the circles of ripples that they made. Water bugs skimmed across the surface, and every now and then a jumping fish would send out bigger circles to meet our little ones.

"I caught the biggest one," I said, grinning at the picture in my mind.

"You did," said Grandpa with a nod of his head.

"You caught the most," I went on, "but I caught the biggest."

"And we had yours for dinner."

Fried in butter and seasoned Mama's special way. It made my mouth water just thinking about it.

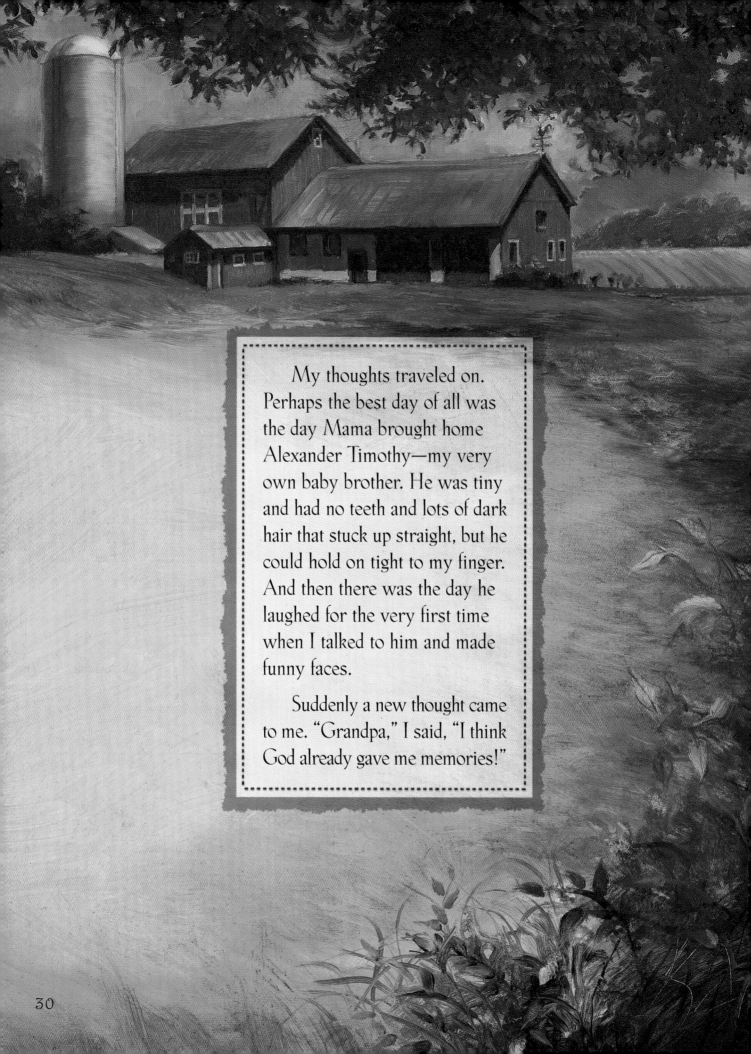

My thoughts traveled on.
Perhaps the best day of all was
the day Mama brought home
Alexander Timothy—my very
own baby brother. He was tiny
and had no teeth and lots of dark
hair that stuck up straight, but he
could hold on tight to my finger.
And then there was the day he
laughed for the very first time
when I talked to him and made
funny faces.

Suddenly a new thought came
to me. "Grandpa," I said, "I think
God already gave me memories!"

Grandpa smiled his easy,
understanding smile. Then he
reached out to rub the top of my
head.

"You know," he said, "I
wouldn't be at all surprised." His
arm pulled me up against his knee
again.

I smiled back at him. "And
I'm going to make lots, lots more,"
I added. "Now that I know the
secret."